Racism is
My Sto
Clive He

Racism is Real. Copyright © 2020 by Clive Henry

This book is dedicated to all the people
that continue to fight for truth and justice.

To my Mother, father, sisters, close
friends, children, and worldwide supporters.
Thanks for keeping me mentally strong over the
years.

We must learn to live together as brothers or
perish together as fools - **Martin Luther King Jr.**

Contents

Introduction - 4

Chapter 1 – September 9, 2015 - 6
Chapter 2 - 70's Soul - 8
Chapter 3 - A father's wisdom 14
Chapter 4 - The world on my shoulders -20
Chapter 5 – Confidence - 25
Chapter 6 - Bad Boy - 30

Photographs - 34

Chapter 7 - The Oracle - 50
Chapter 8 - Making a mountain out of a molehill - 57
Chapter 9 - Social Media - 74
Chapter 10 - Playing the part of a girlfriend - 83
Chapter 11 - Out on Bail - 93
Chapter 12 - Racism is Real – 100

A few people to study - Black History – 103
My contact details - 106

Introduction

They say God gives his hardest battles to his strongest soldiers.

I understand that now, having experienced a life that would have broken most spirits.

I've been trying to write this book for a long time. So much has happened to me in the last ten years. I've experienced so many painful things. From the deaths of family and friends, to seeing the senseless deaths in the media from police brutality. I see how fragile life is. I've just been living day to day, trying to survive and rebuild my life.

We all have a destiny. The main thing I've learned is to turn negatives into positives and to evolve as a human being.

I've changed some names of the people in this book to protect their privacy, but I have included all the relevant information to highlight the struggles and racism we go through as a people.

There are so many people to thank that helped me in life. I cannot name them all, but know that, your love and support is truly appreciated. Even, the people that didn't help. You made me.

Racism is Real, is the reality we as Black people face every day. My story isn't unique in that sense. Just in the sense of me fighting back, and not becoming a victim.

Love and light to all people. Let's heal the world.

Chapter 1
September 9, 2015

It feels like I'm bleeding, laying here on this blue plastic mat. Staring at these gloomy stone walls in this police cell. I'm having so many morbid thoughts. We hear about so many deaths in police custody. I don't know if I will get out of here alive. I'm also, wondering when the duty solicitor will arrive to arrange my bail. The police advised I could make a statement, alone, before I was put in the cell, but I decided to wait. I don't trust their words against mine, and would rather have an independent legal witness in the room.

I got arrested at 2:45pm. My fingerprints and D.N.A sample were taken. I then had to wait in line to be booked in. I've been stripped of anything that could harm me while I'm alone in the police cell. My shoes, my belt, and all of my personal possessions have been confiscated, and held in police storage.

I've been arrested and accused of two counts of rape by my current girlfriend, and the mother of my daughter. This false allegation is so surreal. I feel sick to my stomach. My head is spinning, as the stone cell walls suffocate me. The room is dark with only a small dim light and a thick iron door. I don't know what time it is because I don't have my watch on. Every second feels like an hour. Every hour feels like a day. My mind is racing with so many questions.

The main question is, "how did I get here?"

Chapter 2
70's Soul Child

I was born on a cold winter's night in Nottingham, England on November 23, 1972. Nottingham is the city famous for the legendary outlaw Robin Hood. My parents named me, Clive Wayne Henry. The name Wayne came from my father's love of John Wayne western films.

My very first memory was of me waking up crying. I was a clingy baby. I loved my mother so much and was often found right behind her. My mother had this trick she would play on me. She would stuff her night dress with clothes while she got on with the house work. I would think she was in bed with me until I tried to see her face, hugging the fake body, only to realize I'd been fooled. She got me every time!

I was a curious child. Always asking questions and driving my mother crazy with questions. When I discovered the concept of God. I'd ask questions like, "Who made god? What was god's real name? What does god eat?"

I was also a television addict. Like a sponge absorbing everything and mimicking things I'd seen on the screen. I was like the robot Johnny 5, from the Short Circuit films.

I was the sixth and last child of my Jamaican parents. They came to England in the 1960's for a better life. Part of the Windrush era. When Britain invited people from the commonwealth to help rebuild Britain after the war. No Blacks. No dogs. No Irish. Signs that were common to see in England at the time. Every Black parent knows they have to school their children to the evils of racism in addition to normal standards of raising a child.

I had one brother and four sisters. One of my sisters Carole, died as a baby. She is in the spirit world now watching over us. My brother was fifteen years older than me. He was living his best life. I didn't see him much. All of my young memories are with my sisters.

I remember so many fun times in the 70's. We had hot summers then. It was a time of minimal technology. The technology of the day was our black and white T.V. I remember using gold lucozade wrapping paper to imagine we were watching programs in colour, dreaming we had a colour T.V. ...things people take for granted today.

I was very impressionable. I did so many Mr. Bean, stupid things as a child. It was like living in an episode of The Cosby Show. I remember watching a cop show, with somebody hanging on the top of a car roof. So, you know I had to try it! As a result, my parents would beat me so many times for nearly killing myself.

I remember touching the hot iron face, after my mother told me not to. She had only left the room for a split second. I was curious as to why I shouldn't touch it. I burnt my finger and got in trouble.

I remember watching athletics on the T.V and trying to copy a hurdler, using one of my mothers's dining chairs. I fell flat on my face as my foot got caught in the chair.

It was a happy childhood for the most part. With a few happy scars from my antics.

The things that hindered my life as a youngster were my health problems. I suffered with nose bleeds and tonsillitis. The doctor did advise my mother to have my tonsils removed, but my mother refused, as it was a risky operation in those days. I only had my tonsils removed when I was 24 years old. My health has been great since.

My painful childhood memory was the fact I was one of the smallest kids. I was also skinny. I was teased constantly about this. The other kids on the block would call me a starving African child.

I was teased so much, it caused me anxiety my whole life. The mental torture gave me low self-esteem. I never really felt handsome.

When I look back on my life this negative was a driving force to help me to overcome any obstacle as an adult. Turning my wounds into wisdom.

I can remember many days playing in the back garden looking at insects in detail. Seeing how busy ants were, and being amazed with the tiny world within a world.

We had a Rhubarb plant in the garden. Each year the Rhubarb plant would grow and my mother would harvest this plant and make a Rhubarb crumble pie - which was enjoyed with custard or ice cream.

Unlike now with all the processed food. Most people would cook meals from scratch. My mother was an amazing cook. She created magic every time.

The 1970's were full of beautiful soul music. With so many solo artists and groups gracing the radio airwaves. It was a lot different to now. Music was an emotional and spiritual experience. Unlike the visual spectacle it is today. Artists really had to have talent and great songs for their talent to shine through. So many artists and classics have stood the test of time from the 1970's, so you will understand where I'm coming from. A majority of Hip-Hop songs came from samples of the 1970's musical legends like James Brown and Parliament-Funkadelic.

The Jackson 5, Marvin Gaye, James, Brown, Al Green, Motown, the list goes on. We also had a lot of Jamaican music in my house. Bob Marley, Gregory Isaacs, and Jimmy Cliff, were a few names I can remember. My parents never forgot where they came from, and gave us a variety of music to listen to.

Chapter 3
Father's Wisdom

My parents were married for 28 years before my father died in 1983. I remember two loving parents working together as a team. Sharing household chores and duties. There were arguments too, but not many.

My parents were deeply religious. They weren't diehard church goers, but they practiced what they preached. I remember my house was a welcome home for children and adults alike, from every race without exception. The value that we are all God's children has been instilled in me. I was always taught to help others.

My father was a mechanic. He worked for the famous Raleigh Bicycle company. He was very good with his hands. So much common sense and problem-solving skills. I would often watch him fixing his car. I would try to help out while passing him tools. I had a bike and a go-cart. My father would supervise me, but would let me experience solving the problems myself. I had a happy childhood. Playing with my friends. We would go for bike rides, play football and cricket in the street. So many happy, carefree memories.

Jewels of knowledge and wisdom were drip fed to me. My father would always make me think for myself. His line was, "You don't just have a head to wear a hat." My father was a firm believer in letting a person learn by experience, but would also guide me from real danger.

I can remember watching many wildlife, crime and comedy television programs with my father; like David Attenborough - Columbo, and Laurel and Hardy. He would let me know a few educational things about what I had seen. My father loved horse racing and boxing. Often letting me pick a horse for him. I was his lucky charm. I would pick the horse by numbers; I had no idea of form.

My parents were big on education, even though they weren't academics. My parents were gods of common sense. They wanted the best for us. I remember the first time I was able to touch the Reader's Digest encyclopedias. "Clean hands - Only," my parents would say. There were three volumes bound with a Black cover, with gold writing. Those books covered every subject in the world that we know. These books really were the spark to the intelligent mind I have today. Encyclopedias were the Google of the day.

I always had a higher reading age than my actual age at school because I was exposed to so much educational material. My parents gave me a good balance of education and entertainment. I was such a television addict when I was a child, but my parents also made sure I read to them each day.

My sisters would take me to the cinema often. I remember the first film I watched at the cinema. It was Bambi. The cute deer story. The film that blew my mind was released in 1977. This film was Star Wars. I've been a fan of science fiction ever since. I love the action and the unknown.

I remember my dad being so proud of me. I was in a school play. I played Edmund in the school production of "The Lion, the Witch and the Wardrobe." I received so much praise. I went on to play a small part in a Christmas Pantomime at The Nottingham Playhouse. I was one of the children from There was an old woman that lived in a shoe.

We didn't have much as a family. Money was tight. I remember my best Christmas. It was 1982. I asked for a Matchbox Race and Chase toy car racing game. It featured a police car and yellow corvette car on a track. I remember hours of fun with my dad, playing along; each with our own controller. Racing the cars around the track. Little did I know - this would be the last happy Christmas in my life.

I never take anything for granted. I try to live a positive life. I valued the time spent with loved ones. The last time I spoke with my father was on the morning of December 26, 1983. He was drinking coffee. My sister was a nurse in Leicester, and my father and two sisters went with him to bring her back home for Boxing Day dinner.

Unfortunately, on the way back my father had a stroke in the car, while driving back. All four of them could have died. They pulled over to flag somebody down to get help. There were no mobile phones in those days, and with-it being Christmas, the streets were empty.

They managed to flag someone down. His passenger drove his car, and he drove my father's car to the hospital. Only to find out that his father was also in the same hospital, on the same ward, and later died on the same day. Call it coincidence. Those were unbelievable odds.

Me and my mother got the call with the bad news. My mother was making dinner at the time. Looking forward to a family meal that never happened. When we got to the hospital. My father was in a coma in the intensive care department. He lay there in bed unconscious with monitoring equipment and a breathing tube. It was painful to watch my father laying there, not knowing if he was going to live or die. It just shows how precious and fragile life is. One minute you're talking to someone. The next minute they're no longer here.

December 28, 1983. We were getting ready to visit dad at the hospital in the afternoon. We received a call. Mr. Henry has just passed away! For anyone that hasn't had news of a loved one passing. It's like the scene from Michael Jackson's Thriller; when Michael turns into a zombie and the wall moves out of focus. It's very surreal and a very painful mind jolting experience.

I'm 11 years old. I had no idea that parents didn't live to be old. The man that helped my father and sisters to get to the hospital also had the news that his father passed, around the same time, on the same day!

Family and friends heard the news of dad passing. I never knew our small house could hold so many people. It was the craziest week ever. It was Christmas. There was so much food and drink in the house. Plus, people brought food and drink with them. In Caribbean culture, when somebody dies, people sing songs, bring food and give counsel. My mother was so grief stricken she did not attend the funeral. My father was buried on January 4th, 1984. My life now changed forever.

Chapter 4
The world on my shoulders

I went back to school in January, 1984 - very angry and very quiet. My father had just transitioned to the spirit world. I thought only old people died. My father was only 51 years old. I had to grow up fast. The pain never really goes away. You learn to bury it, like the coffin, covered with the dirt of reality. I was so scared that my mother would die too. I learned how to carry some of the burdens to make my mother's life easier. My mother at this time worked in a food production factory, and it was a very hard manual job.

Me and my sister, a year older than me, took care of our own ironing, and did as many chores we could do around the house. My mother was so strong, but we didn't take that for granted. I had a gaping hole in my heart, but vowed to remain strong to help my mother, as she had to work hard to play both parents.

I felt so alone for years, but had to keep sane for my mother's sake. Being weak at this point would only end with another death. I could not afford to lose my mother.

I tried really hard at school, kept my head down and got good grades. I became very withdrawn. The death of my father made me very introverted.

I had big dreams to be a cinematographer. I wrote off for literature and went to the library weekly. Entertainment and the film world were my escape from the painful teenage world I was living without a father. My father figures at the time were people like: Muhammad Ali. People I remember my father respected when he was alive. My father and I would spend hours watching boxing. It was 15 rounds then. No hype. People slugging it out, and being masters of the craft. My father says he could have been a boxer. I believed him. I saw him in action once in a dispute with a neighbour. My father was a nice man, but he had a temper that you didn't want to see.

Entertainment was the only thing that kept me sane during my teenage years. I watched films most days on VHS video. Steven Spielberg and

George Lucas films were favorites. I started to study the film industry hoping to become a cinematographer. I even applied to film school in London. I had to give up that dream when I discovered my mother would not be able to afford the school fees for film school.

I decided to pursue another dream - music. At school I was part of the Caribbean Steel Band. The band was led by a Caribbean teacher that looked like Quincy Jones, the music producer. He was very strict with hours of rehearsal. Perfection was his thing. Losing his temper, if we hit the wrong notes. Doing school tours and events around Nottingham and the midlands. We had a great experience.

Music was always a big part of my life. I remember from a very young age spinning the records on the family record player. So many talented artists. So many classic records. The first record I bought for myself was by The Police. The group, the artist Sting started with. My sisters would buy music every week. I can remember when I fell in love with Hip Hop. The Sugarhill Gang released, Rapper's Delight, a sample of the record "Good Times" by Chic.

In the late 1970's and early 1980's Hip hop and Dancehall music really started to get popular. Massive speakers. New electronic sounds and special effects would be booming from cars and houses. The youth of the day also had street parties. Outdoor music for free while kids danced in the street.

It was a friend of a friend, from a dance hall sound system that really got me into music production. My friend always looked out for me, giving me free music. He was a gadget white kid, kind as hell, and he knew music; like a librarian knows their books. Such a kind hearted guy. Lending me computer games like Atari, and so much music, from every genre.

My teenage years were lonely. I remember I would walk the streets with my Sony Cassette player, hoping I would bump into a stranger to make a new friend. I decided to immerse myself in music and studying everything, from the business side and music production. I wanted to be a record producer or artist, I still wasn't sure, but that kept me sane and busy. I cannot deny the healing power of music. It got me through some really tough times.

I was at the library every week. Learning about composing music and music production. I even read musician autobiographies, for inspiration. I was self-taught. I had all the time in the world to learn my craft.

My mother helped buy equipment. I also got a job in a pizza restaurant to get money to buy music stuff when I was fifteen. My part-time job was washing pots

Music to me is where art meets common sense. Pop and Hip-Hop music was mainly four-four timing. Meaning four beats in a bar. It's basic math. I got really good, because I could program the drums. Then tap out the musical parts and change the notes to the correct notes to make sure the song sounded like the hits of the day. I spent many hours practicing, and did want to be part of the music industry, but the cards I was dealt in life made me realize, you can't always follow your dreams.

**Chapter 5
Confidence**

In 1987 I was 15 years old.... Studying hard and minding my business. I never had an interest in girls, because I felt ugly from being teased as a child. What made things worse is, I tried to get a girlfriend once at junior school. I was about eight or nine, but failed. I got her number from the phone book. Back in the day everyone had a landline, and the phone number was public information, along with their address. I called her and asked her to go out with me. She said no. When you're a shy child, facing rejection feels like the end of the world. It was like falling into a black hole never to be seen again. I decided then not to ask another girl out.

When I was about thirteen years old and was attending secondary school I had no idea cupid would hit me with his arrow. It was love at first sight. I couldn't get this girl out of my mind. Every time I saw her at school, I would get sweaty palms and freeze. All I could do when she passed me was smile or say a quiet hello. This girl looked like Beyoncé, before Beyoncé was

Beyoncé. She had aura, an angelic face, amazing body, and was way out of my league. I didn't know her name, as we had never had a conversation before. All I knew is she gave me a feeling that nothing had given me before. I had the biggest crush. She wore sky blue Farah trousers and a white school shirt. I would have been stuttering like George McFly, from the Back to The Future films if we spoke. She was always on my mind and a comfort to daydream about, during my painful teenage years. I knew I had no chance to be with this girl. It was just a fantasy.

The fantasy died soon after, when she left my school. Until one day, her best friend pulled me to the side and said my friend fancies you. I was like, "which friend?" It didn't cross my mind that she was talking about my dream girl, because she had left that school to go to another school. I thought I had lost her forever. She says my friend likes you. I automatically thought this was a practical joke, but on the one hand my mind exploded with excitement. I passed her my number and told her to give it to Vanessa. Call it fate or destiny. I guess what is meant to be in life, will be.

A week later I arranged for Vanessa to visit me. She came with her friend to my mum's house, and all three of us were in my room talking. I was so nervous, and couldn't believe, the girl of my dreams was in my room. We had a good conversation for a few hours. I was on cloud nine for days after they left. Daydreaming at school. Vanessa arranged to see me the week after, but this time she came alone.

The date was September 3, 1988. It was the best day of my life up to this point. Me and Vanessa talked, and exchanged our first kiss. From that day forward I was a changed man - and we became an item.

We did everything together. Going out. Staying in. Talking on the phone for hours. Trying to hang up. You put the phone down first. No - You put the phone down first. We would say. We had a spiritual connection and were so in tuned with one another, and so in love. I think when you experience teenage love it is a magical time. No bills and no real-life worries, as you're living with parents. Vanessa was a rare diamond. She is the only girl that I have met with a beautiful body and a kind heart. Very down to earth, and humble. The kind of girl that you could take anywhere.

As time passed, Vanessa got pregnant. She was only 15. I was 16. Both children. We were so young, but so much in love. I was there for all of her pregnancy cravings. Vanessa was the best thing that ever happened to me. Before Vanessa, I was shy with no confidence. Now I felt alive and on top of the world. I was in love with my childhood sweetheart, and things were taking a turn for the better.

Our son was born on the hottest day of the year, July 12, 1990. I was overjoyed, but sad that I missed his actual birth. I was a pizza chef at the time and was on shift when the call came in. Nobody knew about my private life. So, it was a big shock to my co-workers.

My first argument with Vanessa was over my Paula Abdul poster. My hot girl was jealous over a celebrity poster. I reassured her. The funny thing is I didn't even like Paula Abdul that much. I preferred Janet Jackson.

One proud moment was when Vanessa won a Miss Nottingham Modeling competition. It was a Pirate Radio event, at a nightclub. Before the event, I gave Vanessa all the loving support I could give. She was nervous, but I helped her believe in herself. I knew she had the looks and personality to win, as it's about character as well as looks. It was a magical moment, and an amazing night.

For six years me and Vanessa stuck by each other, but had many ups and downs. Part was us being so young; part was my insecurities of not committing 100 percent to Vanessa. I still wanted to pursue music, and I was still worried about my mother, who sacrificed so much for me. I felt I had to make sure she was living okay. For the most part having a lady like Vanessa on your arm is a yin and yang experience. I was admired and hated at the same time. Guys would often tell her lies about me being with other girls to break us up. There was so much pressure. It took its toll on the relationship. We decided to split in 1994, after a make or break holiday to Turkey. We had two weeks together, but were still arguing. They say, if you love somebody let them go. I decided to let go, so she could be happy. I had too much mental baggage. We still had a son together and I would always love her and be a part of his life. When I look back, I wish we were strong enough to stay together. I have never experienced that kind of love again. I know Vanessa really loved me. We are still close friends to this day and she will always be family.

Chapter 6
Bad Boy

A relationship breakup can have its positives. I was reflecting on where my life would go. I badly needed to change jobs, because I had no social life working at the Pizza restaurant. So, I applied for jobs. Eventually, after many applications. I was accepted into a retail environment, by the national firm "Bankrupt Clothing Company"

When people talk about being reborn. This was the chapter of my life, when I was reborn.

Being thrown in at the deep end, in a public environment serving customers, being busy. I gradually began to develop my true self confidence. I was always good at whatever I put my mind to, when it came to work, and quickly became a valued member of the company.

The manager gave me a project to manage to improve stock levels. I had to collect data and submit my findings to the directors after four weeks. My manager believed in me so much, he didn't check my work on the train to the meeting, with the board of directors. This is the level of trust I've seen people have in me over the years, and why I always try my best, in everything I do.

I was organized and produced a chart showing 31 days horizontally and jean sizes vertically. The information was so clear that the directors were able to see what sizes and how many days it took to replenish the stock. Through my efforts, they were able to fix the replenishment problems and maximize on sales.

I was now single. I had a social life. The year was 1994. New Jack Swing was about to explode, and so was I.

One thing I've learned about the mind is, things can lay dormant for years, but alcohol and the right conditions can bring things to the surface. All of my bottled-up emotions from my childhood would make me party like a Rock star. Every other weekend, when I didn't have my son. I would be out - drinking. When you work in retail, there is always some party or promotion on, and I was always invited, because

I was a funny drunk - making guys and girls laugh and have a great time. I made friends with every door man in the city, and they all would give me a queue jump pass. I really was living a Rock star life.

Nottingham, famous for Robin Hood is a small city. Everyone knows people by name or by face. Because I dated Vanessa for 6 years. I was well known. I also worked in a shop where everyone bought jeans. I was about to find out why, ladies loved cool Clive!

I have so many great stories with the ladies. In those days we had pen and paper. No mobile phones to get girls phone numbers. It was all about landline phone numbers. The attention I was getting was unbelievable. I remember I dated one girl who told me, "I'm only sleeping with you because you're popular." I had now become a player. However, I wasn't the kind of guy that lied to women. I was always upfront with my intentions, giving choice, so nobody got hurt. It was all about safe sex.. fun. My nickname was 192 directory enquiries, as I had a big black book, full of phone numbers. Whatever I do, I always try my best. I would chat to girl's way out of my league, some too tall, some too pretty, just to see if I could get them. Like Bobby Brown, when he was the underdog, I had a lot to prove. I was making up for all the years I was teased as a child.

In the early nineties my role models were people like Bobby Brown and Tupac Shakur, both underdogs that really surpassed people's expectations. It was so true of myself. I did so many things and went to so many places. I was very liked by people.

From 1994 I lived a rollercoaster life of booze and partying. Making friends and going to other parts of the country, parts of Europe, and New York City, to visit family. Life was happy because it was fast. I had no time to reflect. I don't know what happened, maybe I got bored, but I decided it was time for a change in 1998.

Mum and Dad - Wedding photograph - 1963

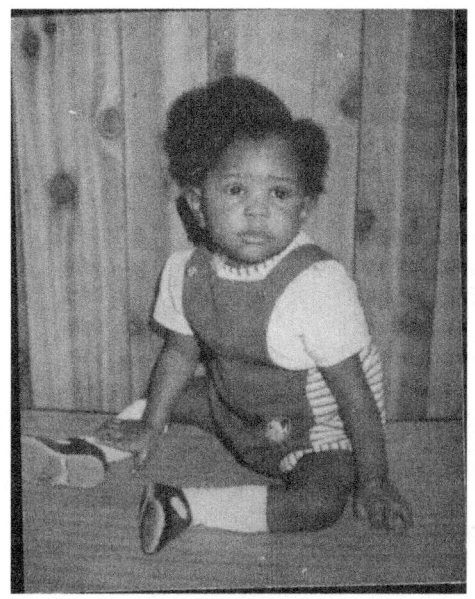

Me at 1 year old - 1973

Me at junior school - 1980

Me with my Bobby Brown haircut - 1989

Vanessa - My childhood sweetheart - 1988-1994

Vanessa - The mother of my first born and my life confidence coach <3

Holiday in Marmaris, Turkey - 1994

Holiday in Falaraki, Rhodes - 2003

My white t-shirt selfie - 2009

News photo that went viral on the internet - 2011

Visit to the British Museum, London - 2009

Me after court with UPS - March, 2010

Holiday in Las Vegas, USA - 2011

Me, tired from doing legal paperwork - 2017

Selfie before work - Taxi driver - 2019

Me in my Columbo t-shirt - 2020

Chapter 7
The Oracle

It was 1998. I had just spent four years in retail. It was a time of great fun and laughter, fast living and women, but now I wanted more money and a change of direction.

May 26, 1998 was the day I started working in the UPS Customer service department. There was 4 weeks intensive training. Then it was straight onto the phones, and into the war zone to solve problem package queries.

Over the years I got really good. Understanding through study and experience how everything worked. I quickly got promoted to a specialist department. There I managed around 50 queries per day. Talk about busy. I learned to multitask at a high level. Working around the globe dealing with queries by time zone and priority. In the morning it was the Far East, and in the afternoon, it was Europe and the Americas.

One day I was asked to do a presentation for the sales department, to help them understand the workings of the parcel service - so they could advise customers to get better shipping practices, and thus, gain more business.

After my presentation. They were so impressed with my PowerPoint presentation, that they asked me to join the sales team. I decided to accept the offer, and was grateful for a new challenge.

My first year in the sales team was quite difficult. It took many hours to master my craft. However, I had an advantage of knowing how the whole system worked, so I was often asked for my expertise on queries that my sales colleagues had. We traded information. I got sales techniques and they got query guidance. It was then I was given the nickname, 'The Oracle.' This is the name of the Black lady, in the Matrix film. Little did I know that destiny had a path for me to cross with the real oracle, author, Sophia Stewart.

Around 2002, my eldest sister was diagnosed with breast cancer. It was caught early. She had a mastectomy to stop the cancer spreading. I thought the worst would happen. Cancer to me at the time, meant death. We did everything we could to help my sister. I attended chemotherapy appointments. Took my sister shopping, and did just about everything in my power to help make her life easier. It was such a stressful time, and I admit I would drink on the weekends to drown my sorrows and try to ease the pain.

With my mind being out of sync, this was the start of my downfall. An old girlfriend that had been in and out of my life had contacted me again. She was living in a small bed-sit type apartment. She says, "We should be boyfriend and girlfriend." At the time it sounded really good. However, I was about to find out why actions speak louder than words. This girl had friends that were having babies, and it looks like I was selected to be "the sperm donor" for my new girlfriend. A term she used on me in a future argument. I was love bombed so badly. So much love and affection, until she became pregnant. After about 3 months, her mask fell off.

We went to the cinema one evening. On the way back, she decided to argue with me. She ran into her flat and locked the door. No matter how much I banged on the door or shouted through the letterbox, she would not let me in. It was dark and cold and I had to get a bus home that night. She wouldn't return my calls and I never heard from her again.

February 22, 2003. I got a call from her mother. She had a baby boy. My third child. I also get letters from the child support agency, and they start to deduct money from my salary. I made contact with my old girlfriend. We had to talk. So much had happened, but was never resolved. When I did visit, she had a new boyfriend, who had been dating her since she was pregnant at around 5 months. I felt so used and abused, but for the sake of the child I decided to be civil. I used to have my older son every fortnight, so I decided to have my new son every fortnight, from eight months old, so he could bond with me and his brother. We also sorted out the money side of things, so the money went directly to my baby mother.

Could life get any worse? Yes, it could. After the breakup of this relationship. I was still drinking heavily. I met another woman. This time she already had a son, around 9 years old. She told me she didn't want more children, and was on the contraceptive pill. This wasn't a serious relationship, but I foolishly trusted her word. My mind was foggy from everything that was going on in my life. She became pregnant. I stayed with her. My fourth child was born on January 16, 2004. Another son. This baby mother was in love with her first baby father. It didn't take long for this relationship to fizzle out. From 3 months old. I also had my new son every fortnight at weekends, to bond with me and his other brothers.

For years I had my sons every other weekend. Bonding with them and trying to be a good father. Life was stable until my legal problems started with UPS.

November 13, 2006. I took an offer to work in London for UPS, covering an Account Executive's maternity leave. I still came back on the weekends I had my children. I also still helped my mother and sick sister to get her shopping and help them with anything I could. Life was busy, but I made the sacrifice for my family.

I was a Field Sales Account manager. Servicing high spending accounts, growing new business and helping the customers get the best out of the service. When you look back on your life. You can see the destiny jigsaw. Ten years before, around 1996. I met a guy on a Saturday night in Nottingham. We were out drinking. This guy asked for bars we could recommend. I saw he was alone, so asked him to join us. I didn't know who he was, but I love to make people feel welcome and help others where I can. I kept in contact with him over the years, and he was the one that gave me a cheap room to rent in London. Treating me like a little brother. He was wise and cared for me like the brother I never had in my life.

Just when I thought things couldn't get any worse, my mother had a meningitis scare. I came back one weekend, and saw one of my sisters with a sad look on her face. I asked, "Where is mum?" She replied, "She's in the hospital." Thoughts of my dad came flooding back, Thinking the worst. I went to the hospital straight away. When I got there, my mother had drips and cables around her. She said they were doing tests. I was so relieved to see her alive, but so depressed to see her like this. My mother was my hero, and the strongest person I know. We couldn't get an answer on when she would be going home.

My assignment in London came to an end in November 2007. My mother being sick helped my decision to return to Nottingham. More money was good, but family is priceless.

I started back in my old role as an Inside Sales Executive with UPS in Nottingham, in November 2007.

Chapter 8
Making a mountain out of a molehill

The date was October 8, 2008. I was called into the office by the manager, Peter. He became the new manager after the UPS merger with Lynx couriers, when my old manager, Tina was promoted.

Peter says he is putting me on a Performance improvement plan (PIP) to help me regain lost business. I had never heard of such a thing. I left his office and read the paperwork. I noticed there was no signature from the Human resources department. At this point I had worked for UPS for 10 years, H.R had always signed off on any changes regarding employees, no matter what.

The room was spinning as I went back to work, as I was so confused on what had just happened. I was asked to supervise the merger in my department from January, 2008 until July, 2008. The conversion of lynx accounts to UPS was 95% effective. I helped manage 30 staff to educate, register for online shipping (using my ID and password for thousands of accounts), and collate all the data on a weekly basis. It was a massive task. I didn't do my regular job during this time. There was nobody more qualified than me in that department. I knew my job inside and out. I had the nickname, The Oracle, like the Black lady in the film The Matrix, and I lived up to that name.

At the end of the day. I decided to go to see the manager. Everyone had left the office. I knocked on the manager's door. Peter said, "come in."

I sat down and asked, "Why have you put me on this Performance Improvement plan, when you know that I supervised the merger in this department?"

Peter said, "This is to help you gain lost business." I replied, "You saw me at the management meeting, stating how important this merger was, and that it had a 95% success rate of companies being retained and turned into UPS accounts. Peter wasn't making sense talking about lost business. There was no lost business. This project was all the department was doing for 6 months. A mammoth task. I said, "When I'm wrong I admit that I'm wrong, but when I'm right, I will fight it all the way." I thanked Peter for his time, and left work.

From that day forward, my life changed forever. The department sales target of £3,000 was set for me to achieve in October. I worked really hard and did £3,100 in sales that month. After achieving this I thought, I proved my point. Little did I know I was going to get the shock of my life. The manager gave me a sales target of £4,000 for November. This was very odd, since the yearly sales plan ends in October. This target was discrimination, as there was no other person on a target that was compulsory, never mind as high as £4,000. When I didn't bring in the amount, I received a letter from Peter, advising I would have a disciplinary meeting on December 21, 2008. It had been 2 months of hell, and now was just about to get much worse.

December 21, 2008. A few days before we broke up for the Christmas holidays. We had the meeting to discuss my results for the past two months. There were four people in the room. Me, the manager, my supervisor, and a work colleague. Me and my colleague sat opposite the manager and supervisor on a small table.

The manager started off with my results, saying the £3,100 I achieved in October was satisfactory, but the £1,800 I achieved in November was unsatisfactory. Me and him went around in circles verbally while I disagreed, and gave my reason why I thought I'd done my job. I asked the manager, "Am I the only person on this PIP?" What happened next changed the game. The manager raised up out of his chair slamming his hands on the table and shouted, "No. You're not the only one" (an action he denied doing in the court documents). This action right here, made me realize, this was personal, and the manager did not like me, for whatever reason. I laughed, because seeing this in the corporate world was a joke to me. I grew up in Saint Anne's, Nottingham. A ghetto area, with real ghetto characters. There was nothing to fear in the corporate world, in the form of violence. Peter, then after sitting down advised I would be getting a written warning. I replied, "You can do what you want, because I'm going to appeal it." The manager's face looked shocked. The room went silent. The meeting ended, and I went back to work. A few days later. We broke up for the Christmas holidays.

I had the worst Christmas worrying about what had happened at work, knowing the manager was trying to force me out of a job. Returning to work on January 5, 2009. The supervisor came up to me and handed me a letter while I was sitting at my desk. I opened the letter and what I saw shocked me. It was a written warning letter. The shocking part was the letter looked like it had been deliberately smudged and put into the envelope. It was like getting the wind knocked out of me. I quickly passed the letter around to co-workers in the same section. I asked the whole department, "If they were on a Performance Improvement plan2 (PIP), they all said, "No." So, the manager was lying. It was my first day back to work, so nothing productive went on. I left work deflated, and could not stop thinking about the nightmare I was having. That week I put in for an appeal of the written warning, and was advised it would happen in a few weeks.

I woke up the next day. Pains in my chest, and I couldn't breathe properly. I called the doctors surgery to get an appointment. I thought I was having a heart attack. Looks like the anxiety and stress had made me physically ill. I went to see my doctor, showing him the smudged warning letter from work. The doctor looked disgusted with what he'd seen and what I'd explained. He documented the details and signed me off work for two weeks. I told him, "I can't take two weeks off because I have an appeal hearing". I took the week off to try to relax, hoping that this nightmare was just one bad manager. UPS had been good to me for ten years. I was so looking forward to resolving this.

The hearing date came. It was taken by my old manager, Tina. I started to explain what had happened, and showed her the smudged warning letter. She was shocked. Tina said that was probably an accident. Tina also said after listening to me, that she would investigate the situation and come back to me within four weeks. I went back to work, as normal.

Three weeks later, I'm at work sitting at my desk when I get an email from Kathy in H.R., at the same time I see Peter, the manager come out of his office putting his jacket on, and looking smug, like he had just heard some good news. I opened the email from H.R and read it a few times. I could not believe what it said. After the appeal investigation. The decision was to, "remove the written warning, but put me back on the PIP, with realistic goals." I saw red, but kept very calm. No wonder the manager was looking smug. I printed a copy of the letter. I showed it to a work colleague. I told him, "Let them have their moment of glory, because the shit is going to hit the fan after lunch".

I got back to my desk and sent an email to H.R, asking to reply with the corporate office email for UPS in Atlanta, Georgia, U.S.A?

Five minutes passed, and just like clockwork, I get a phone call from Kathy in H.R, with panic in her voice asking for us to have an emergency meeting. Ten days later we had this emergency meeting.

On the day of this meeting I really had enough of the whole situation. In this meeting were Managers, Tina and Peter, Kathy from H.R, me and a work colleague.

Tina asked, "What was my problem?" I started to read the warning letter to them..., "Remove the warning, but put me back on the PIP with realistic goals." Before I could finish, Tina told me to ignore that line. I looked at her in shock. I said, "Ignore that line?" I then went into a barrage of facts about me being a worker for UPS over ten years, with 7 years - 100 percent attendance and an accolade of praise from customers and other UPS workers worldwide. I told them this whole experience feels like I failed my 3-month probation period. After my speech. Tina apologized. Then made Peter apologize to me for the pain he put me through. I replied with, "I don't accept your apology". It wasn't genuine. They were trying to contain the problem in-house, because I asked to escalate to the corporate office. The way I saw it. Things had gone from bad to worse, because now more people were involved, not to resolve the issue, but to brush this under the carpet. I abruptly told them, "This meeting is over". Please can H.R get me the corporate details I asked for, to escalate this higher. H.R. gave me the corporate details to raise my grievance higher.

I sent the grievance complaint to the London office, and followed it up with an email a week later to confirm receipt. I received an email reply, the lady in question, which I was told was the H.R. manager replied with, "Yes. I received your complaint. What do you want me to do with it?" I was in total jaw dropping shock. This complaint was in-depth, with all the information to make it crystal clear. What had happened and that this needed investigating from higher management. I quickly had a look at the company directory on the UPS intranet, to see this lady's position. To my surprise she was not the H.R. manager. She wasn't even listed. I was so angry. What I did next was book a day's holiday that Friday. I decided to raise a case with the employment tribunal. I was getting played by UPS from all sides.

Friday came and I found the tribunal office. May 8, 2009. I was given an application form to complete. I also attached a copy of the documents with the complaint to UPS. I asked the clerk, "Once completed. How long before a case is open?" He told me, "If the case is valid. It normally takes three business days to open a case." On May 14, 2009. The tribunal case was open. UPS received a copy of this document. Now the complaint was official, and the war had just begun.

For the rest of 2009 I was under so much pressure. Not from my daily work, but from the tension in the air. The Jay-Z quote comes to mind, 'How to move in a room full of vultures.' My every move was watched. UPS had their spy's, trying to get information from me. Subliminal goading messages were said by co-workers and management, but I kept my cool. Knowing that when the tribunal case court date came up this hell would be over. The year ended better than 2008, because I knew it wasn't long before I was free of this place.

The New Year started. Here is 2010. I'm made to have a desk outside the management office. I guess to keep an eye on me, and to play psychological games with me. I was given an area to manage, which performed well on its own. The area was Kent, South East of London.

Just when I thought my life couldn't get any worse, my mother had a heart attack. At 73 years old, I thought the worst. Thinking my mother was going to die. I couldn't believe this was happening. This is when I learned how to be strong, because that was the only choice I had. My mother had heart surgery, and I couldn't tell a soul at work. I had to present a daily poker face.

Making sure in my moment of weakness and distress, my pain was not used against me. I had to feed my mother for a year, after the operation, and make sure she had taken her medication. I managed all of her house duties to nurse her back to health. I had to be strong for her, as well as myself.

As the tribunal court case progressed. Paperwork between me and the court went back and forth. I didn't get a lawyer to represent me because I didn't have the money, and this was such an open and closed case, in my eyes. All the evidence was there in documented form. I understood legal things from working in the other departments. There was no way
UPS would not be found guilty of discrimination - I thought.

I got some good news. I received a letter from the tribunal court, giving me the dates for the court case. March 23rd until March 25th. I couldn't believe there was light at the end of the tunnel. I quickly put in my letter of resignation. Stating that my last day would be March 19, 2010. It was a funny day. News traveled fast in my department that I had resigned. I'm a man of integrity and principles. There was no way I would work with people that had little value for life. My working life was destroyed by one man, while everybody watched and did nothing. The lesson I learned here was trust actions, never words.

The day of the court hearing day came. It was a nice spring day. I was accompanied to court by an old work colleague; Sandra had been a witness to all of the madness that happened.

In the courtroom. The UPS managers were there: Tina, Peter, and Anthea, with a Black female lawyer. I felt, what a hypocritical move.

The UPS lawyer went first in asking questions. She was very aggressive in her approach, but it didn't faze me. I knew what weight I held in the case and the documented evidence, and was soon to embarrass them when I asked my cross examination questions.

UPS wrote I was the lowest performer in the department. I used their lies against them. Yes. I was the lowest performer, because I managed the merger. This makes logical sense. For anyone with a brain. You wouldn't let the lowest performer manage a mammoth merger project, if they were inexperienced. You also wouldn't let that person slide for six months, doing no work in a sales environment. Under cross examination with the manager, Peter. All their lies were exposed. Everyone in the department used my Internet logins to register people for shipping parcels. With numbers in the tens of thousands. It would look like I did the merge myself, without the help of 30 coworkers. My name was on every account as I.T support. Then the court was adjourned. Sandra was excited as we waited in the meeting room, and saw how I exposed UPS. Lies are lies, no matter how you jazz them up. The thing is UPS forgot that everything was documented in Black and white.

We were all called back in the courtroom. The tribunal judges told us after deliberation. They concluded that UPS were not guilty of anything. The judge also got my name wrong. He called me Mr. Harry. On hearing this, I felt my blood boil, from the pit of my stomach. I didn't say a word. The UPS team looked happy with the result. This was my first experience of court. It would not be my last.

A tribunal is a closed court to the public. I'm sure if a jury was involved, this result would have been different. I vowed to myself, that I would fight to appeal this decision. I was now unemployed. My world had fallen apart, and I had nothing to lose. My main thinking was I have to fight for the people, that companies destroy, and to show others to fight for justice. If they could do this to me, a great worker, they could do this to anyone. Weeks later I received the written judgment with one statement. As the tribunal put it, "I'm making a mountain out of a molehill."

My mother always had a saying, "Where there's breath, there's life." This was my reality. I lost everything, but was still breathing to see another day.

The first thing I did was to register as unemployed to receive social security money. After that was taken care of, I decided to use all of my brain power to legally fight this injustice I had received from UPS. I had meetings at law centres and citizen advice center's in Nottingham. I also started to study the legal side of my case, to get to appeal the decision. I lost track of how many emails I sent, books I read, and companies I contacted that dealt with judicial complaints.

Months had gone by. No luck on all of the doors I tried, but one magical thing did happen. In April 2010, when I was at my lowest point. I made contact with Nelson Mandela's office, in South Africa. The iconic activist that spent 27 years in jail, only to come out and become President - and change South Africa forever. I sent an email outlining my case. I didn't think I would get a reply, but I understand the power of one person believing in you, to motivate you, to follow your dreams. The email response advised, "Mr. Mandela had retired from public duties, but advised to keep fighting for justice" I gained unlimited strength from that reply. This was a living legend and activist that made a difference on this planet. A man I respected. I thought, if he can go to jail for 27 years and come back to become President, I can fight this case.

September 17, 2010. I had a meeting with my local Member of Parliament (M.P). I went through my case that afternoon, and he was sympathetic to seeing that I got an Appeal hearing, at the Employment Appeal Tribunal in London. He wrote a letter to them, and I was granted an appeal hearing on February 2, 2011. I was also allocated a legal representative to put my case forward to the judge on the day.

On the day, ten minutes before the hearing. My legal representative had a 5-minute meeting with me and my sister, who came with me for support. He said, off the record, "Even though you have been treated badly, "I can't talk to the judge for you." He then left. Here I go again, having to represent myself. As I explained to the judge what had happened, I could see the pain and empathy for me in the faces of the court admin and usher. The judge, after hearing my case, told me he isn't going to overturn the judgment. I told him, "I will not stop until I get justice."

From October, 2010 until September, 2011 I continued to work for the local council, as a Business Development manager. Making over £100, 000 in sales. I managed parking contracts, waste bin contracts, skip hire and confidential waste for the Commercial Services department. This agency job was great, because while still fighting my case through legal channels. I had an outlet to keep busy and gained confidence that I still had skills to do a great job. A permanent role did come up for this position, but I think the council discovered I had a case with UPS. Back to the unemployment line for me. I lost the job.

At this moment in time. I had the European Commission court open a Human rights case for me, and the Court of Appeal in London. The Court of Appeal had just closed my case, letting UPS off. I now started to realize, there really is no justice for Black people. No matter how strong the evidence is. Look at the Stephen Lawrence case and the Macpherson report, I thought. The Lawrence family was still fighting for justice twenty years later. This is when I decided to use social media to expose them all.

Chapter 9
Social Media

In September 2010, after months of knocking on legal doors to make complaints about my legal case I decided to expose UPS though social media as I was getting nowhere through the gatekeepers of the Ministry of Justice, The Office for Judicial Complaints, the Employment Appeal Tribunal and the Court of Appeal.

I set up the Facebook group: Justice and Racism in 2010, and wrote:

Clive Henry Vs UPS Ltd

I worked at UPS Ltd for 11 years, with 100% attendance for seven years. I had NEVER received any disciplinary action before.

In January, 2008 I was asked by Manager A to supervise the merger of all the Lynx Courier accounts in our department.

In July, 2008 Manager B who was the director at Lynx couriers became my manager.

In October, 2008 I was placed on a Performance Improvement Plan (PIP) which was never authorized by HR.
I hit the £3000 department monthly target. This was raised to £4000 the next month. I was shouted at and given a written warning on failing this target. I was also given a smudged warning letter. I was signed off with occupational stress because of these events.

The warning was revoked after my appeal, but I was advised in writing, that I would be placed back on the PIP, with realistic goals.

I emailed HR to escalate to the corporate office. I was quickly contacted by HR to arrange an emergency meeting at this point. UPS HR and management were trying to cover this up.

In that meeting I was told to ignore being placed back on the performance improvement plan At this point I raised a grievance. I again asked for the corporate office details, but was given a false HR contact.

The Race Discrimination Tribunal hearing was on March 23, 2010. I represented myself, as I thought it was an open and closed case. I resigned from UPS on March 11, 2010.

I was the only Black male and only person EVER to be placed on a PIP.

UPS are an official supporter for the 2012 Olympics, and an equal opportunities employer. I am fighting an appeal after the judge dismissed the case in a perverse way.

The judgment given has vital information missing to paint a different version of events. Thus making the employer look innocent of wrong-doing.

This is when I had to face reality, and found that the law doesn't always do the right thing. Even if evidence smacks them in the face!

I made contact with every organisation on the planet and received good advice to take this further.

I requested the judgment and written reasons to raise an appeal against this decision in May, 2010.

The appeal was opened on July 3, 2010. I waited 8 weeks for the appeal tribunal to close my appeal on September 1, 2010. This is when I opened this Facebook group page.

At this point I also made contact with my MP, who contacted the tribunal, along with myself. This was on September 21, 2010. The tribunal received my letter on September 22, 2010 and was quick to reply on September 23, 2010 - advising the appeal has been reopened (surprise, surprise)!
In March, 2011 an investigation is open with the European Commission for Human Rights and the Court of Appeal has a case open.

Within a week of setting up this Facebook group page. I got a letter from UPS's solicitors, threatening - If you don't remove this Facebook page within 10 days, they "may take legal action" ... At this point in my life. After everything I had been through. Scare tactics were not going to work on me. I decided to expose UPS to let people know the truth. I felt it was my duty to help others realize the reality of racism that we were living in.

I went one step further. I posted the letter from UPS's solicitor on Facebook for all to see. Masking the address details. I had mixed reviews. Some people told me to take the page down, as they were worried about my welfare. I told people I'm not taking the page down. May, in legal terms didn't mean anything. As time passed, people saw that UPS's threat was a bag of wind. I knew what I held from the UPS legal case documents. They were guilty. If this case was put before a jury, they would have been found guilty. The tribunal is a closed court and I'm sure some corruption probably took place.

They say it only takes one match to start a forest fire. I was about to become a forest fire.

I decided to make the case go public, after the court of appeal closed my case. The first news publication I was in was called Fight Racism - Fight Imperialism. A national newspaper in the United Kingdom. The next one was Minority Perspective online newspaper, The Voice newspaper, The Afro News, The Black Presence, and Hinterland Gazette, based in Atlanta, Georgia, USA. Newspapers that highlight things from the Black community. I did contact every mainstream newspaper in England. However, I was ignored.

Twitter was also in its infancy at this time. I thought here is another tool I can use to get my story out. I started to tweet the news links about my case, the news was met with attacks from trolls, as well as sympathetic people. My account got hacked. I realized I'm going to have to up my game. This is when I decided to set up ten Twitter accounts. All under the name of Racism is Real 1 to 10. I figured if any got hacked, I could still get my messages out.

I was now a force to be reckoned with. I was unemployed at the time, so used every waking hour to tweet the information on all accounts. There were days when I never left the house, bathed or shaved. I looked awful and felt awful, but I was hell bent on getting the truth out there.

I targeted different groups. Celebrities, Human Rights groups, companies, legal types, and newspaper groups worldwide.

It was the most surreal time of my life, when people started retweeting the information, sending it around the globe in its millions. So many people helped me, big named celebrities, too. I found there are good people in this world that want fair treatment, and justice for all, regardless of race.

I also did many radio interviews with various people in the UK, America and Canada. The Dr Vibe show reached out to me; this show was an online radio podcast show. I had a sixty-minute slot to tell my story. This radio interview really made a difference. I used the audio link for this show, and used Twitter to send this around the globe. It was the biggest download in the show's history. There were many that heard the show that became followers of me on all my social media accounts. Words are powerful. One lady advised the radio interview had a bigger impact on her, than reading the articles about the case.

During this social media war. I was still fighting a legal battle, by the case being with the European Commission, and later with the European Court for Human Rights. I wanted to show people that, you have a voice. No matter how small you think you are. I had accounts on Facebook, Twitter and Instagram. All under the name Racism Is Real.

I remember going into the city. I saw an old UPS work colleague. He said, "You're everywhere, like MasterCard and Visa. It was funny, but I was dead serious about showing people the evils that we as Black people face in the workplace, far too often without a voice.

With my story going viral. I had many followers. From people I admired to just any person on the street. I made sure I highlighted in radio interviews that UPS would not allow me to spread lies, and would sue me if I was wrong. The thing is, by now UPS knew what damning evidence was in the documented court bundles. UPS had to just let me be with my social media exposure.

I know from feedback that I opened many eyes and minds, with what I did. I was also told that policy changes happened within UPS.
In my mind I had lost everything, so had nothing to lose. I helped others see how wicked the law and these corporate companies could be. Social

media was also a sense of healing. I was able to vent and educate at the same time.

In 2012 there were high profile cases with people dying in Police custody. The Trayvon Martin case really hit home. Will Black people ever live a life that isn't filled with stress from the cradle to the grave?

In 2013 the group called Black Lives Matter was formed. This was a global group born from the pain and destruction of Black life. It did not take me long to join the group in Nottingham to help. As I saw it. I'd experienced racism first hand in the workplace and within the legal system.

I did a few protests, but had to survive. This was when I got back into work, and couldn't commit to the group. I wanted to be my own boss, so I wasn't ever in the position again where my life could be destroyed by a manager. This is when I did research to become a taxi driver.

Chapter 10
Playing the part of a girlfriend

It was late in 2013. I had just finished a mammoth battle with the UPS court case and social media marketing awareness campaign.

I received a message from Debbie, an ex-girlfriend I dated in 1998. We had a casual affair. We split when she became pregnant and I wanted a D.N.A test. Her friends told me, "She doesn't know who the father of the baby is."

We split and went our separate ways and I never heard from her again, until now.
Debbie claimed my daughter wanted to know if I was her father. I was also curious to know, as at this point I had three sons, and the suspense of not knowing if my daughter was mine or not had been eating at my soul for years.

I paid for a D.N.A kit and did the test with my daughter. Weeks later in January 2014, I received the results via email. The test came back positive. Finally. I could now try to build a relationship with my long-lost daughter.

I told my family. They too were excited about the news. I quickly set up a family gathering, with my mum, sisters, sons, my daughter and her mother.

Everyone was so happy with the new edition to the family. I started to see Briana, each week. Trying to make up for lost time. I felt so guilty that I missed her growing up. I had 3 sons that I saw grow from babies to young adults. My daughter was very quiet and withdrawn. I knew it would take time to develop a bond. While all this was going on, I became very close with her mother again, we were older and wiser, I thought, so we decided to try to make a relationship work. Leaving the past in the past.

I took my daughter to school and picked her up in the afternoons. With her sister and other friends. I was unemployed and looking for work, so I had a lot of time on my hands to bond with my daughter.

Debbie explained that she suffered from bipolar disorder. I didn't really know what it was, but gave her all the support she needed during our time together. She was often at the doctors, taking a lot of medication, and needed constant reassurance. There were crazy mood swings, but nothing could prepare me for what was coming.

Debbie became pregnant in July 2014, and continued to work as a mobile hairdresser. That's what she told me, she did. I was very confused as she had no hairdressing equipment, never spoke about work; I never dropped her to work as she always got a taxi.

I decided one day in August 2014, to find out where Debbie worked. I had the location of the work address from Facebook messenger, when it used to give a person's location, so I was able to pinpoint the address.

That morning. I left Debbie, before she went to work. I parked at a nearby pub, went across the road to the hair salon I could see, and asked if Debbie was working today? They told me they don't have a Debbie working there. I left confused and went back to the pub, bought myself a cola and decided to wait.

Within minutes, looking out of the window. I see a taxi pull up. Debbie gets out, goes to the shop and goes around the back of the building. Wow, I thought. Where does she work? And, what is around the back of the building? I saw Debbie walk back to the shop to buy some food and then she returned around back.

Now I'm really confused. I start to look up and see a sign and a phone number. With my Columbo mind, I decided to Google the phone number. Bingo. I got the website up. It was for a massage parlour. I navigated the page. To my shock horror. I see Debbie on the website, as one of the ladies working there. I also read reviews, about the girls working there. It was more than a massage. Debbie was working as a prostitute. I felt sick to my stomach with the deceit. No wonder she never left me be alone with my daughter. So, I didn't ask too many questions.

I waited in the pub all day until I saw Debbie waiting for a taxi. I sent her a WhatsApp message, asking how her day was, making her laugh, and acting like I hadn't just found out her big secret. We agreed I would see her later that night, and sleep over.

Later that night, we were in bed. Now was my time to reveal all. I told her I followed her to work today. She got upset and cried crocodile tears. I asked her, when were you going to tell me? When we were walking down the aisle? She said she wanted to tell me, but couldn't. I felt badly let down. I had been deceived, and all trust had been broken. We broke up. Debbie was pregnant. I did try to contact her, but she ignored me. I told my family that we broke up, but did not tell them the reason why.

April 13, 2015 - Debbie gave birth to a baby boy. She made contact through a friend to let me know. I was excited, but at the same time, in pain. Me hoping this would have a positive outcome. I asked Debbie to do a D.N.A test to prove the baby was mine, and felt every right to this because she had deceived me. I helped out with the baby, but there was no relationship.

Along with her sister and brother, we decorated Debbie's new house for a few months. Coincidently, we had a massive row when the house was finished. I had received a message in error from Debbie to one of her friends, that she was just keeping me sweet to take her mother to Wales for a holiday. I was now a Taxi driver and had been since November, 2014. So, she planned to use me.

September 3, 2015. I went to see Debbie later that evening. She asked me to help move a few boxes to her new house, from her mother's house. I agreed to help. The car was full with stuff, to the brim with boxes everywhere, including on top of my daughter. The baby was also in the car.
When we unloaded the car. My daughter, who had her tonsils out the week before decided she wanted to go back to her grandma's house to sleep. I dropped her off, and then went to the shops to buy some milk, bread and a bottle of beer. After the day I had a small 330 ml beer was needed.
Me and Debbie were still arguing, but decided to call it a day.

She decided I stay the night. Debbie had a bath first, and then I had a bath afterwards. When I finished and went downstairs to the kitchen. I saw Debbie had poured my bottle of beer in two glasses. I didn't want to cause another argument, and it was only a tiny amount 165 ml each. Debbie was smoking a cigarette at the back door. There was just me, the baby, and her in the house. She hadn't moved in yet. The two dogs she owned were at her mother's house.

We decided to go to bed. We were in bed talking and cuddling. One thing led to another and we decided to have sex. When we finished, I put the baby in the middle of the bed to sleep comfortably, as he was in the baby car seat carrier.

In the morning, Debbie and I had sex again. It was Friday September 4, 2015. I had to work later that evening. Weekends are where a Taxi driver makes most of his money. I left around 9am and went home.

Loving messages were exchanged between me and Debbie all day Friday. On Saturday September 7, 2015 I received a very strange and angry message from Debbie telling me to stay away from her. I was very confused, but thought I'd give her a few days to think. The bipolar disorder gave her crazy mood swings.

The day my life changed was September 9, 2015. I had just done a taxi job to Derby and went to my mother's house. When I pulled up outside my mother's there were two police cars. The officers advised me to park my car and come to sit in the police car. My mother and sister were there staring, not knowing what was going on. I didn't know what was going on. I thought they were there to ask me questions about a neighbour that I did a taxi job for a few weeks prior, and was on a tag curfew. She said the police might contact me, because she went past her curfew time after being caught in traffic coming back from a wedding.

I was offered a seat in the back of the police car. I wasn't handcuffed. The situation was calm. The officers and I were calm. The officer then said, "We're arresting you on suspicion of an alleged rape of Debbie" .... I said, "My girlfriend." The officer read me my rights. I was then escorted to the Nottingham, Bridewell Custody Suite to be booked in until I was bailed.

The time was 2:45pm. I'm there in the police station with a long queue of people, also waiting to be booked in. shouts of abuse, and banging from unruly detainees. When I got to the desk, they took my fingerprints and DNA. After finally booking me into a cell, I had to remove my belt, shoe laces, tie, and all of my personal effects.

I was put into a cell. Dimly lit. Greyish blue stone walls, a thick metal door, with a small hatch at the top. I felt so sick to my stomach and confused, I just lay on the padded blue mat with my coat over me to keep warm - wondering how I got to this point, and will I get out of here today. I opted to wait for the duty solicitor to be present while the police conducted their statement interview. After what I went through with UPS. I sure didn't trust the authorities. I wanted to make sure there were independent eyes so my statement wasn't changed.

Charlotte, the duty solicitor, sent for me and we went into a private room where she introduced herself. She advised she had read the victim statement, and it is very unlikely to progress to a case, under the circumstances. She read out the victim's police statement. I was in total shock at the time, with the lies I was hearing. Charlotte stated. There are two charges of rape. One on

Thursday night and the second on Friday morning.

After this meeting. I was escorted to the police interview room to make my statement. The two police officers introduced themselves, the solicitor was present. They recorded the interview on the data recorder. I gave my statement in full detail, and offered the police to check my Gmail account while there, as I had an app on my phone that recorded all of my text messages. I wanted to show them the loving text that Debbie had sent after the alleged rape. The police declined though. The interview ended. I was allowed to collect my belongings and was sent on my way.

Chapter 11
Out on Bail

I finally got home after being in a police cell for 8 hours. I hadn't eaten all day. I felt like my stomach had fallen out and this lasted for 2 years. I honestly know there are many innocent people in jail from my experience. The legal system is a very flawed system, dealing with Black people in the worst way.

From my arrest on September 9, 2015 and bail conditions denying contact with Debbie, directly or indirectly. Debbie tried to
contact me multiple times, from her own phone and through her friends. I reported these to the police, who gave me an incident number. The police did nothing until.

September 21, 2015 - Debbie comes to my mother's house in a taxi, but nobody answers the door. She quickly left and I reported this to the police. On September 24, 2015 the Police went to see Debbie to warn her about contact and confiscated her mobile phone. Does this sound like a person that was raped?

I had to submit all evidence to the law firm that could help my defense. My health declined. I suffered from anxiety, weight loss, and heart palpitations with stress from the case, and my future being in limbo. I went to the doctor to explain what I was going through. He advised under no circumstances should I contact Debbie again, even if this case is dropped. He says she sounds like she is going through a psychotic episode and could cause me harm.

I had to take so much time off work because there were days when I couldn't focus. My stomach felt sick no matter what I ate or how I tried to forget about what I was going through. As a taxi driver. My first concern was for the safety and welfare of the public. There were days when I couldn't concentrate and couldn't get out of bed, feeling suicidal. It is the worst feeling in the world to be falsely accused.

Every few months I had to visit the police station to sign off on my bail conditions. On September 6, 2016 I was charged - to my surprise, with two counts of rape. Things took a turn for the worse.

I had to apply for legal aid to pay for my legal representation as I didn't earn enough. Documents went back and forth until my first court date to plead not guilty at the magistrate's court came up on October 6, 2016. The following month, in November, I had to go to the

Nottingham Crown court to plead not guilty again, where the final court trial date was set for July 3, 2017.

I met a barrister, who was my advisor for the day at court. Me and my best friend were there in one of the court meeting rooms. He told me, from his experience he doesn't think this should ever have been a case, as he had looked at the information. He told me I would be represented by Barrister Wright, who wasn't there that day, but was very good.

The New Year passed with this still hanging over my head. My defense team sent court documentation to the court stating that the CPS should declare the accuser's mental health to the court. A deadline was set for the end of February 2017. The CPS did not send the requested information to the court, by the deadline date. This is when I started to question everything.

March comes and I start to question Bethany, my solicitor working on my case. I was frustrated that the deadline was missed, and after multiple calls and emails to her, all she could tell me is that she had asked the CPS to disclose the relevant information to the courts. This went on for months. I even went to the office to speak in person. I told her to get a court order for the CPS to disclose the information. After all. It was my life that was in limbo and the stress and frustration was making me feel depressed and weak. Because I had dealt with legal processes with the UPS civil case, I studied the process of my criminal case closely. Trust nobody was my motto.

I raised a formal complaint to the director of the Law firm, stating I was not happy with the service, and how Bethany was handling the case. Bethany wasn't getting the court order to get disclosure from the CPS to shut this case down. She also stated that the court date had changed, but couldn't give me details when I asked for the new date in writing. I found it very odd. Here's me having to fight my own defense team to defend me. The director came back to me by letter trying to explain things away.

I wrote back and advised I don't want Bethany on my case, and I want you to change Barrister Wright. The barrister assigned to my case in November 2016, had never met me, sent an email or letter to introduce himself. When was he going to meet me, on the day of the trial? This was not normal.

June 13, 2017. I was assigned a new barrister. I met her at the Law office. The first thing Lucy said to me after introducing herself was, "Did you meet the other barrister?" I said, no. She looked at me in shock. We then went upstairs to discuss the case.

I had prayed for someone like this. The new barrister was sharp, very experienced and seemed thorough and results driven. I learned a few things that day. There were notes in the case, from the CPS, probably sent in error with Facebook conversation from Debbie talking to a friend. In these conversations, Debbie mentioned she had been raped by her witness, and six other guys. The medical examination stated there was no evidence of her being raped. The barrister went through the case notes with a fine-tooth comb, to clarify all points. She concluded that Debbie's statements did not add up and the CPS had not disclosed all the standard information that they should have. The barrister stated she will get the court order to get disclosure from the CPS. I left the office feeling way better than I had done for the last 2 years, with this nightmare hanging over my head. I told my family about the new barrister meeting and said if she is as good as I think she is this case will be closed within 2 weeks.

June 27, 2017. I'm sitting on the toilet, minding my business. My mobile phone rings. I got a call from the law firm office. Sally told me, "I have some good news and some bad news." My heart sank. I said, "What's the bad news". Sally said, "There isn't any bad news! The Crown Prosecution Service has decided to drop the case.

We need you to come to court in the morning to formally close the case."

I was ecstatic. It was one of those moments when you have to pinch yourself. I quickly finished on the toilet and let my family know the good news. It was like the biggest weight lifted off me.

The next day at court. I was dressed in suit and tie waiting to go in, not knowing if I was going to have to speak. I sat at the back. The judge spoke. My defense spoke, but stated nothing to add and then the prosecution spoke briefly. Stating new evidence had come to light, and therefore they would not be pursuing the case any longer. I didn't say a word. The whole process lasted about five minutes. The judge said I was free to leave the room. I went back to the waiting area. When my barrister came out the room. We went to a meeting room and had a brief conversation. She told me if I have any dealings with Debbie in the future, regarding the children, this must go through legal channels as Debbie would be very upset and this approach will eliminate more trouble or court cases.

I gave Lucy a Thank you card, with a gift voucher inside. She thanked me, saying, "Nobody ever gives me anything." I told her," thank you. I prayed to god and you showed up." She said, "Now you get back to your life, and good character."

I went home. The two-year nightmare was finally over.

Chapter 12
Racism is Real

With everything I experienced. I really started to look back at the origins of racism. Many people believe that Black history started with Slavery, and this is the narrative that you learn in school. However, in the age of information, and access to the internet, ignorance is a choice.

According to science, life on this planet started in South East Africa around 200, 000 years ago. Mankind migrated, and populated the whole planet. There are D.N.A gene markers that track this, showing we are one human family. Climates and gene mutations may have affected the way people look.

Africa is the centre of the world. Even though the educational and media propaganda machine tries to paint an alternate reality. Africa, which has 54 countries, and is the second largest continent on the planet gave the world everything we have today, and this is where the celebrated Greek scholars like Plato and Socrates were educated.

The transatlantic slave trade was the foundation for racism and all of the tools of religion, mind control, and torture were used to give Europeans the benefits of capitalism.
The western world system is set up to disadvantage people of colour. Black people have been dehumanized so we don't expect to be treated fairly. This has been programmed into our mindsets for over 400 years. The negative stereotypes serve as programming - internal and external to destroy Black lives. We see this in the media, the judicial system and in education.
From sun up until sun down we worked until death. We were given scraps. We were separated from our families. Lost our mother tongue and were told to obey our masters in the Christian bible. We suffer from cognitive dissonance, and have been stripped of our unity and trust for other Black people by the psychological methods of Willie Lynch, an English slave owner.
Though my story is a painful one. I have gained wisdom, healing, and spreading love and knowledge where I can, via social media.
Racism is race prejudice, plus social and institutional power. So, all the systems serve a purpose to enforce the stereotypes about Black people and is an invisible force controlling our lives. If you search the dictionary for the definitions of Black and white, you will see the

stereotypes are highlighted for negative and positive programming.

I could go on forever, but I will say this. If my life journey can open any minds to see the reality we live in and improve race relations, I would have done my job. We have to want better for ourselves and our children. Nobody is going to save us apart from us.

As we heal and learn about our past. We will gain knowledge to fix our future. Information is power, when executed. We have to unlearn all the lies we have been taught and look at our brothers and sisters as family. Once this happens, we will go back to our original essence of - it takes a village to raise a child. Then maybe humanity will understand, "You can't hold a man down without staying down with him." - Booker T. Washington

A Few People to study Black History & Knowledge

Robin Walker - Black History Matters
Jane Elliott - Blue Eyes/Brown Eyes Anti-Racism Experiments
Ashra Kwesi
Brother Polight
Dr. Ray Hagins
Minister Louis Farrakhan
Shahrazad Ali
John Henrik Clarke
Michelle Alexander - The New Jim Crow
Yosef Ben-Jochannan
Dr. Phil Valentine
Dr. Booker T. Coleman
Dr. Runoko Rashidi
Dr. Joy Degruy
Neeley Fuller Jr.
Stephen Lawrence - The Macpherson Report
Nelson Mandela
Malcolm X
Lee Jasper
Zita Holbourne - Activist
Lee Jasper - Activist
Maxie Hayles - Activist

- KRS-One - Hip Hop Scholar
- Martin Luther King Jr.
- Muhammad Ali
- Harriet Tubman
- The Black Panther Party
- Marcus Garvey
- Nat Turner
- The Great Groit
- Assata Shakur
- Mansa Musa
- The Dogon Tribe
- Seneca Village aka Central Park
- Tariq Nasheed - Hidden Colors - Film
- Dr. Frances Cres Welsing
- Ida Wells
- Maya Angelou
- Toussaint Louverture - The Haitian Revolution
- Rubin Carter - The Hurricane - Film
- Dr. Claude Anderson - Powernomics
- Black Wall Street
- Windrush Scandal
- Bob Marley
- Patrice Lumumba
- King Leopold II
- Timbuktu Manuscripts
- Roots (TV Mini-Series 1977)
- Thomas Sankara
- Rosa Parks
- Hannibal Barca
- Dr. Umar Johnson
- Eric Thomas - The Hip Hop Preacher
- Frederick Douglass

Black Inventors
Willie Lynch
Imhotep – The world's first multi-genius

My Contact Details

Instagram: racismisreal
Skype: clivehenry2
Zoom: Cliveh26@gmail.com
Twitter: @clivehenry1 #racismisreal
Facebook: Clive Henry or Racism is Real
Email: cliveh26@gmail.com

For published information about my case, including
news and radio interviews
Google: Clive Henry UPS
Or

Clive Henry The Dr Vibe Show

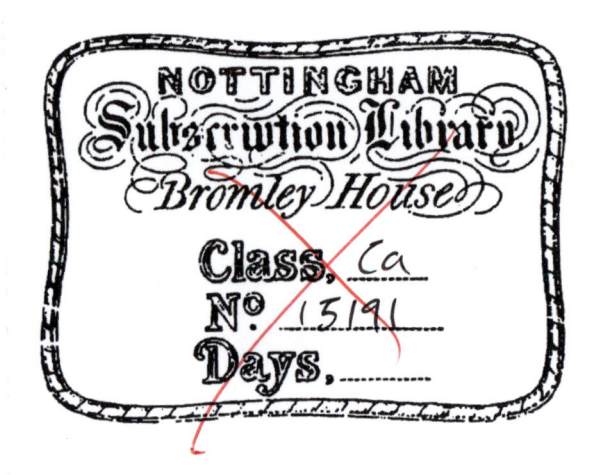

Printed in Great Britain
by Amazon